The Fighting Red Tails: America's First Black Airmen

by Warren Halliburton

Illustrated by Jon Gampert

cpi
contemporary perspectives, inc.

Library of Congress Number: 78-13173

Art and Photo Credits

Cover illustration by Jon Gampert
All photographs in this book were provided courtesy of the U.S. Air
   Force. "Official U.S. Air Force Photo."
Every effort has been made to trace the ownership of all copyrighted
material in this book and to obtain permission for its use.

Library of Congress Cataloging in Publication Data

Halliburton, Warren J 1924-
   The Fighting Red Tails: America's First Black Airmen

   SUMMARY: A history of the 332nd Fighter Group, an all-black
flying squadron which achieved recognition for its combat proficiency
in World War II.
   1. World War, 1939-1945 — Aerial operations, American — Juvenile
literature. 2. World War, 1939-1945 — Afro-Americans — Juvenile
literature. 3. United States. Army Air Forces. 99th Pursuit Squadron
— Juvenile literature. 4. United States. Army Air Forces. 332nd
Fighter Group — Juvenile literature. [1. World War, 1939-1945 —
Aerial operations, American. 2. World War, 1939-1945 — Afro-
Americans. 3. United States. Army Air Forces. 99th Pursuit Squadron.
4. United States. Army Air Forces. 332nd Fighter Group. 5. Afro-
American air pilots.] I. Title.
D790.H25   940.54'49'73   78-13173
ISBN 0-89547-061-6

Manufactured in the United States of America
ISBN 0-89547-061-6

Contents

Chapter 1

The Red Tails Join the War

"Go get them!"

Colonel Davis was yelling into his radio. It was June 9, 1944. Davis was flying a P-47 — one of the best fighter planes in the skies. The colonel was talking to his fighter pilots. Their small, fast planes were grouped around some bigger, heavier bombers. These were the American B-24s. Davis's fighter group had to keep the big planes safe.

The B-24s were on their way to bomb the enemy. They would hit the Nazi oil fields at Munich, deep inside Germany. But just now some enemy planes had seen them. Four German fighters — ME-109s — were diving at the American bombers.

One of the B-24 pilots looked up at the fighter planes flying around him. "Our guys better do the job!" he called to his copilot. "Am I nuts or is every one of our fighter pilots *black*?"

"You're not nuts," answered the copilot. "You're not color blind, either. And be happy, man, be happy! That's the 332nd Fighter Squadron. Those black Americans are the Fighting Red Tails! And if what I hear about them is true, these Germans better get out of here. The Red Tails are out to prove just how good they are!"

The Red Tails heard the order from their leader, Col. Benjamin O. Davis, Jr. Their P-47s lined up for battle. Then they attacked. One after another they went at the German planes. The enemy planes dodged and darted about in the air. The German ME-109s were fast and easy to turn. The battle of the small planes was on — and both sides were ready.

But one P-47 shot past its target and zoomed in front of an enemy plane! In an instant the Nazi was on his tail, firing with all guns. The American pulled back on the stick of his plane. It soared up into the clouds where it was safely hidden from the enemy — but for how long?

In the next moment the P-47 shot back out of the clouds. There was open blue sky all around. There waiting for him was the enemy plane. It was coming in fast, faster — too fast! In a burst of fire the Nazi ME-109 shot right past!

The Red Tail was back in control. Now he let go with his own fire power. The Nazi plane turned and dodged. Another blast of fire came at the American plane — and missed! The American let go with his guns. A hit! The ME-109 burst into flames. The Red Tail watched as the enemy pilot's parachute opened.

The American pilot flew past and joined his buddies. The sky was now swept clean of Nazi planes. The battle was over. He mopped his face, shaking his head. Then he broke into a big smile. This might be just one more air victory to the U.S. Air Force, but it was the first for the 332nd Fighter Group. This had been their first time in battle with the enemy, and it had been a long time coming.

As the Americans let go with their guns, a German plane burst into flames.

Chapter 2

America Trains Its First Black War Pilots

☆☆☆☆☆☆☆☆☆☆☆☆☆☆☆☆☆☆☆☆☆☆☆☆☆☆☆☆

In the U.S. Army black soldiers had always been put in units of their own. Segregated from white soldiers, they lived and trained apart. Until World War II the Army Air Corps took no blacks at all into their pilot training program. But as the war went on, blacks demanded the chance to join the air war too. Finally the army backed down and blacks were allowed to become pilots. But they were trained to fly separately from whites.

Many people felt that black and white soldiers should be trained together. But this idea was a new one. The army felt that with a war to be won it would be too risky to try. Black air cadets were not happy

Tuskegee Institute in Alabama was where the new black cadets were trained to become pilots.

about this segregation. But they felt that some kind of flying school was better than none at all.

Tuskegee Institute in Alabama was chosen as the training center for the new black airmen. Tuskegee was a college for black students started by Booker T. Washington in 1881. It was also the place where the scientist George Washington Carver made many of his important discoveries. Now, in July 1941, this poor but famous college was again making history as the training base for America's first black air corps cadets.

There were just 13 cadets in Tuskegee's first air force class. Five graduated as officers. But they were only the first. Hundreds more would serve as air force officers in World War II. The Tuskegee pilots were put together in their own flying group — the 99th Fighter Group of the U.S. Army Air Corps.

In August 1942 the 99th Fighter Squadron was taken over by Col. Benjamin O. Davis, Jr. The young black men had become pilots of single-engine fighter planes. Now they had to be trained to use those planes in battle. And what better man could the army choose to train them than Colonel Davis? He was the first black man to graduate from West Point in almost 50 years. Word spread among the men of the 99th, and everywhere there were smiles at the name of their new leader.

"Colonel Davis! We have the top man!"

But with their joy there was also worry. Each of the new pilots now knew the job that had been cut out for the 99th. They would have to prove themselves to the world — and to a man like Colonel Davis! They knew it would not be easy.

And there was nothing easy about the training program that lay ahead. It was tough from the very first day. They were learning to fly as a fighting group. Hour after hour they had target practice — split-second turning, firing, diving, and firing again.

Colonel Benjamin O. Davis Jr., (seated in plane) discusses his ideas with the new pilots.

There was a steady stream of flying drills. They would learn the art of falling and twisting to stay with — and *behind* — an enemy plane. Then came the practice for night attacks — weeks of being shaken from sleep to take off and land in the dark. Slowly and painfully, the men of the 99th learned the real skills of war — how to kill and keep from being killed.

At last the day came when Colonel Davis thought the 99th Fighter Squadron was ready for the air battles of World War II. The games were over. It was time for the men he had come to love so much to fight. And Colonel Davis could not help wondering how many of these young pilots would make it through the dangerous times ahead.

Chapter 3

America's Black Air Corps Grows

On April 1, 1943 the 99th left Tuskegee for Italy. Very soon after that they were moved to North Africa. Here they had two main jobs. One was to break up the enemy's camps, keeping their soldiers on the run. They would fly low and destroy as much of the Nazi food supply and army housing as they could. Their other job was to fly along with the big American bombers. They would protect the bombers when they went on raids.

The 99th saw much action in both jobs. They became skilled and lucky. Each mission they went on was a success. Before long the sight of the brightly painted rear ends of their planes lifted the spirits of Allied soldiers fighting the Nazis on the ground.

"Here we go for another good round!" men would cry as soon as they saw the Red Tail planes. "The Red Tails are with us — we'll be sure to win this one!"

Meanwhile three more squadrons of pilots had graduated from Tuskegee. They formed a new and larger all-black air unit. The 332nd Fighter Group would train at Selfridge Field, Michigan. Colonel Davis was brought back, and with him some men from the 99th. These men, experienced and battle-wise, would help train the new men. Then they would return with them to fight in Europe.

The new pilots were already becoming a well-ordered fighting unit. The motto from their training days was "Get to your guns!" It was just one sign of the eagerness and determination of the 332nd.

The 332nd got its orders quickly. Based in Naples, Italy, they were told to patrol the coast. This meant dive-bombing and low-flying shooting, to destroy the enemy's supplies and soldiers. Allied ground troops were fighting around Rome. The Nazi army was on the march across Europe. Destroying their supplies would cut their ground strength. Storehouses for food and

Pilots of the 332nd Fighter Group heard the order "Destroy the enemy supply lines!"

weapons were the targets. But almost from their first day in Europe, the 332nd ran into an enemy that also fought well.

The daily, bloody air battles told the men of the 332nd that they were in for a long tough war.

Chapter 4

Always Expect the Unexpected

The planes of the 332nd were flying low over a large group of enemy soldiers. The enemy had American soldiers pinned down behind some hills. As the pilots prepared to fire on the Nazi troops they sighted an enemy plane. It was still far away. Its pilot seemed in no hurry to help his friends on the ground. Instead, he seemed to be waiting.

Lawrence D. Wilkins and Weldon K. Groves of the 332nd knew why the Nazi pilot was waiting. As soon as they opened up on the enemy below, they would be sitting ducks for an attack from the air. That's when the enemy plane would swoop in on them and pick them off one by one.

Wilkins and Groves left the pack and turned their P-39 airplanes to chase the enemy. Soon the Americans drew within range of the slower Nazi plane. They fired, but suddenly one of Grove's guns jammed. Wilkins moved out ahead and kept firing at the German plane. Groves could do little but move around to frighten the enemy pilot and keep him running.

But now Wilkins saw that there was still another, bigger danger than getting shot in this chase. Their fuel was more than half gone. If they kept after the enemy plane they might not make it back to base. They decided to head for home.

This experience taught the young pilots of the 332nd that there were no sure things. Guns might not work when they were needed. And a new saying was born: "Always expect the unexpected."

Pilots of the 332nd, like Roger B. Brown, learned to make the most of the unexpected. He was flying his P-39 at 2,000 feet. Without warning the engine went dead. Brown was over water with no place to land. He tried everything he knew to get the engine started. But all the while he was getting closer to the ocean. He was only 800 feet above the waves.

Brown was too low and falling too fast to jump with his parachute. He moved with the quick mind of an

athlete. First he took off the doors of his plane and threw them overboard. Then he unfastened everything he could and cut off all the switches. All the while he managed to keep his plane above the water. Now he eased it down. He kept gliding until his air speed was less than 120 miles an hour.

The plane shook like a giant bird as it swiped at the water. Then it crashed. Brown jumped into action. He was out of the plane in less than three seconds. Almost at once he was hit by the tail of the plane. The next second his P-39 sank out of sight.

A passing British ship picked up Lieutenant Brown soon after he made his escape. The sailors could hardly believe he had lived through this crash. In fact, Lieutenant Brown was the first pilot of the U.S. Army Corps to have crash-landed a P-39 at sea and lived to tell the tale.

The pilots of the 332nd were slowly gaining experience. And slowly but surely, the American bombers they protected hit more enemy rail lines and motor convoys. Without these supply lines the Germans were left with little food and ammunition. Soon they had to turn to their cargo ships for help. The 332nd joined other air force groups in bombing and shooting at these ships. The Nazi army was badly weakened. It was no longer able to stand up to the Allied push in Italy.

The enemy troops pulled out of Rome and headed north. Along the way they set up new supply lines and storage centers. Pressing forward, the American ground forces once again called on the Army Air Corps. They wanted ships and supplies bombed. On May 31, 1944 the 332nd Fighter Group got a new job. This time they would escort the bombers of the 15th Strategic Air Force. Great days were ahead for the 332nd. The men felt the promise of adventure that lay ahead for their all-black air group. But with the adventures would come great problems for the 332nd.

Chapter 5

The Tide Turns Against the 332nd

All through the month of June 1944 the 332nd flew with the bombers of the 15th Air Force. The bombing targets were in Italy, southern France, and the Balkans. It seemed that they were meeting enemy planes on every bombing run. Each battle was worse than the last. More and more pilots of the 332nd were lost. The enemy seemed to know the Americans were losing. They fought that much harder, sending new planes to stop the Americans from knocking out their supply lines.

Just west of Aircasea, Italy was a strip of landing ground. It was believed to be one of the Nazi's most important air supply lines. The American army knew that Italy would fall if they could keep supplies from reaching the enemy's front lines. The job of wiping out the supply lines fell to the 332nd.

The American air attack had to be done in a special way. If the enemy learned of it, they would be able to find the P-47 fighters almost immediately. A giant radar network along the Italian coast protected the Nazis against just such attacks. The 332nd Squadron had only one way to keep from being spotted. That was to fly low — too low to be picked up by radar. There was no doubt that the plan was dangerous. But it was the only way to get the job done.

On June 24 the black fighter squadron took off. The big planes flew low. They skimmed just over the waters of the Mediterranean Sea. The weather was bad. Thick, dark clouds blotted out the sunlight. The pilots searched the cloudy skies for enemy planes.

Suddenly the engine of one plane cut out. The plane dipped into the water. Pulling back on his stick the pilot lifted his plane. But the engine failed to catch. The P-47 nosed back down and crashed. It sank almost immediately.

Every man in the group watched in horror but the 332nd continued on. The sea just below was choppy. Now and then a giant wave lashed upward toward

the low-flying airplanes. Suddenly another plane slipped too low. It was slapped at by the waves. The pilot tried to pull up. But the weight of the fuel and bombs made his plane sluggish.

A wing was ripped by water. The pilot jumped out just before the plane skidded and crashed. He was lucky to escape the quickly sinking craft.

One of the other pilots spotted the man in the sea and went after him in a tight 180-degree turn. But a downward gust of air caught his plane. It was thrown into a flat spin. A moment later the plane exploded as it hit the sea. Neither pilot could be seen through the thick, heavy smoke that covered the water.

By this time the 332nd was halfway to its target. But its problems were by no means over. The lead pilot had made a mistake. He had turned east at the place where he should have turned north. Reaching the coast, the planes were more than 70 miles from where they should have been. The lead pilot saw his mistake. He made a 90-degree turn.

But once again fate took a deadly hand. The lead plane was closer to the water than he thought. The pilot saw the water rush up toward him. But it was too late. All at once the plane plunged into the waves. A moment later the giant explosion it made lifted the sea. No trace of the plane was to be seen. The radio was

still. No one said a word as the assistant flight leader moved forward to take the lead.

At last the planes were close to the target. But now a thick fog began to roll in. The pilots could not see the ground below them. As they closed in on the Nazi supply strip the fog got thicker. Nothing could be seen of the enemy. The new flight leader made a painful decision.

"Give it up! Give up the target. We're going home!" he called into the radio.

This was a terrible blow to the pilots of the 332nd. Four good men already had lost their lives on this flight. And for nothing. The enemy had not even been touched!

The next day the pilots of the 332nd answered the call from Flight Operations. Their hearts were heavy but every man knew the flight had to go on. Their job this time was some low-flying bombing of roads in northern Italy. These roads were known to be the enemy's main supply lines for the fighting further south. If they were destroyed much of the enemy's strength would be cut.

The 332nd went to work. Although no one said it, each man wanted to lash back with greater effort today

at what happened yesterday. Perhaps they could somehow make up for the loss of four friends.

The winds were strong and blew against them — stronger than they had expected. Even though the weather was clear, the planes were blown off course. They had drifted well into German sea lanes and found themselves being fired upon from below. An enemy ship was now filling the skies with antiaircraft fire. One pilot said later, "It was so thick . . . it looked like a blanket."

The planes of the 332nd went in on the target. In screaming dives they opened up with all guns on the shell-spitting ship below. It was a Nazi destroyer, big and mean. Before long they had the ship ablaze with fire and smoke. Then another direct hit and the enemy ship blew up. The sea rocked from the terrible explosion. The planes spread in a wide circle around the parts of the enemy ship. Seeing that the ship was sunk, the 332nd went on with its mission.

Once over their target, the P-47 pilots searched the ground. But there were no enemy troops to be seen. They seemed simply to have vanished. The commander ordered the pilots to return to base.

The mission left the 332nd feeling very different from the day before. They had not been able to bomb the enemy from low levels as planned. But they had

taken an even bigger prize. A whole enemy destroyer was put out of the war!

The news of this victory at sea went everywhere. It was cheered wherever it was heard. But the men of the 332nd Fighter Group took their fame with quiet pleasure. These men were no longer eager young boys. Yes, they had now come back from the blow of defeat. And they had scored a major victory! But they were not wild with joy. For now every man in the group was remembering four friends flying with them just one day before.

Chapter 6

The Beginning
of the End

It was clear by July 1944 that Nazi Germany was losing the war. Total defeat was closer every day. The Nazis were fighting harder than ever to keep back the advance of the Allied armies. But theirs was a losing battle. American leaders had planned well.

Just when the war was going well, the 332nd found it had a new kind of trouble. This time it was not trouble from the enemy. It came from within. By now the attacks on Germany's oil fields were in full force. The 332nd was moved to Rametti, Italy. There they were joined by the famous 99th Fighter Squadron — the first black air squadron in the history of the U.S.

Men from the 332nd Fighter Group were joined by the famous 99th Fighter Squadron.

Army. The 99th was to become part of the 332nd. The all-black fighter force would be made bigger and stronger.

But the change was not that easy to make. The pilots of the 99th had fought long and well in the war. The Red Tails were famous throughout Europe. These pilots did not want to belong to a group of flyers they thought were still young and untried.

The men of the 332nd had their own problems with the change. True, they had not fought as much as the 99th. But they felt they were just as able. They were not about to let the other group cut them down. Slowly but surely, the new and bigger 332nd split into two unfriendly camps.

Colonel Davis saw what was happening. He knew that unless his men worked together they could not fight well. This kind of problem could be more dangerous for the 332nd Fighter Group than the enemy. He understood that working out the problem would be up to him. He also knew that to fight well his men had to keep their group pride.

There was only one way, and it had to be done fast. Each man had to be judged by what he did best and what Colonel Davis thought he would be able to do better than any other man. Whatever flying time a man had put in was not important. Whether he was flying two years or two weeks, whatever he could give to this group to make it the strongest and best was the only thing that mattered.

Feelings of old loyalties and the pride of being first to fly had to be overcome. He convinced the men that the only reason they were there was to fight and win

Men from the 332nd learned to work together as a team.

the war. They were trained fighter pilots and their one job was to destroy the enemy, not one another.

The men of the 332nd got the message. And they took comfort. Their number had grown. The group had gained experience. Now they could all see that they had to work together to win.

All this time the enemy was hard at work. They fixed what weapons they could still use to fight. They set up new lines of supply. And they built new supply stations in different places. These now had to be destroyed by the Allies. The American bombers went out on raids seventeen days a month. The new 332nd went along on many of these missions. They fought off groups of enemy planes sent to destroy the B-24 bombers over Rumania, Austria, and Bohemia.

The men of the 332nd came back from each mission with a new story and a new hero. One such hero was Capt. Joseph D. Elsberry. The young officer always seemed to be ready to go into battle. Three Nazi pilots found this out the morning of July 12. Captain Elsberry was leading a fighter group that day. They were protecting American bombers. Elsberry spotted enemy planes coming in. He radioed his men to prepare their ships for a fight. That meant dropping their extra fuel. The planes could move better in a fight if they were lighter.

By this time the P-47s had dropped back. The bombers went on alone to finish their mission. The Nazis saw the gas tanks falling from the fighter planes. They thought the small planes were dropping bombs. So they turned away from the bombers and started after the fighters instead.

But the Nazi pilots made their move a moment too late. By the time they turned away from the bombers, the 332nd fighter pilots were already on their tails. Leading the group was Captain Elsberry.

The captain lined up his gun sight. He fired a short burst. The side of one Nazi plane blew away. But Elsberry kept on its tail. He fired again. The enemy plane went out of control. Then it slipped off to the right and fell to the earth.

A moment later a second enemy plane flashed by. Elsberry rolled his plane in a steep turn. He started firing. The Nazi plane began to smoke. It fell into a dive and plunged to the ground.

As he pulled out of his turn, Elsberry caught sight of another enemy plane. It quickly shot across his path in a sharp dive. Elsberry rolled to his left and went after the plane. Then he started firing. The Nazi twisted and turned the plane to avoid Elsberry. He was a good pilot. But not as good as the American.

Elsberry stayed with him. He followed the plane down to about 11,000 feet. Looking back he saw that four planes of the 332nd were close behind. Elsberry broke off his attack. But the Nazi pilot continued his dive. Down he went, hoping to avoid the American on his tail. Just before reaching the ground he tried to pull out of his dive. It was too late. The plane crashed into the ground. A ball of fire marked the spot where it hit the green land below.

By the end of the month almost all the enemy's oil fields had been bombed by the Allies. Soon there was not even half the oil the Nazi army needed for fuel. This was the beginning of the end for Hitler's Germany. And hints of the next big step were in the air. The Allies would invade Germany itself.

Chapter 7

A Farewell to War and Each Other

"Destroy everything that moves!" was the order. "We are moving into Germany."

The job for the 332nd was to finish their work as well as they had started it. Their days together from the time they were eager young cadets had brought them down a long, hard path. Many had been lost on the way. But those who were left knew that they would now set the stage for the biggest part in the war. An invasion by Allied ground troops was around the corner. And then — *the end of the war!*

The day came when the 332nd was given time out from fighting. There was something going on — something special. Everyone could feel it and the men shared the feeling with winks and grins. Then the official word came from army chiefs in Washington, D.C. On September 10, four pilots of the fighter group were singled out. They were to get awards for all they had done in service to their country.

The ground crew waited each day for their flying brothers to come home.

The day was to be special in another way. Col. Benjamin O. Davis, Jr. was also to be honored. And Gen. Benjamin O. Davis, Sr., his father, was flying in to present the awards. The general was the highest ranking black officer in the U.S. Army.

The men of the 332nd were all "spit-and-polish" as they stood waiting for the general. They stood tall when the ceremony began. They were proud of what they had done as a fighter group — and as America's first black war pilots. And they were proud that they were being singled out for honor by their country. All eyes were on General Davis. He marched smartly up to the stand. Then he spoke to his son.

Brigadier General Benjamin O. Davis, Colonel Davis's father, was asked to present his son with an award.

"I am very proud of you," he said.

Everyone there felt something special pass between father and son. Both had a look in their eyes that everyone understood. Then the general went on to read the army's message to the men of the 332nd.

For extraordinary achievement in an aerial flight as pilot of a P-47 type aircraft. Faced with the problem of protecting the larger bomber formation with the comparatively few fighters under his control, Colonel Davis so skillfully disposed his squadron that the bomber formation suffered few losses.

The following four men of the 332nd also got awards that day:

44

Capt. Alfonso Davis: *He led an attack on an enemy airfield at Grozwardin, Rumania, on August 30. The 332nd destroyed 83 planes on the ground in this raid.*

Capt. Joseph D. Elsberry: *Battled his way to his targets, defeating the enemy in the air and destroying his vital installation on the ground.*

First Lt. Clarence D. Lester: *With complete disregard for his personal safety he destroyed three enemy fighters, thus preventing the enemy from making concentrated attacks on the bombers.*

Lt. Jack D. Holsclaw: *With complete disregard for his personal safety ... with an outstanding*

Lieutenant Clarence D. Lester (left) was congratulated for his courage as a pilot.

display of daring and combat skill, destroyed two enemy fighters and forced the remainder to break off their organized attacks.

Each and every man of the 332nd took satisfaction in these awards. They understood that the honors given to their friends were very much their own. Each man knew he had done his share.

And the men of the 332nd continued to do their share throughout the rest of the war in Europe. Finally, at midnight on May 8, 1945, the fighting in Europe was over. The Allies had beaten the Nazis. The bloodshed and killing on European battlefields and in the air had ended.

And then, once again, on June 8, 1945, Col. Benjamin Davis was honored. This time he was given the Silver Star for bravery in combat. The commanding general of the 15th Air Force said of Colonel Davis: *He is a fine soldier and has done wonders with the 332nd. I am positive that no other man in our air corps could have handled this job in the manner he has.*

The 332nd had been overseas for 22 months. During that time 450 black pilots had joined its ranks. They flew nearly 1,600 missions and over 15,000 air flights. They had proven that color was not important among

The quiet young men who learned to fly at Tuskegee ...
... became a fierce fighting unit in World War II.

fighting soldiers. No one race of people owned the will or courage to fight bravely and win. Nor did any one race of people own a love for their country.

On October 17, 1945, the fighter group was awarded the Presidential Distinguished Unit Citation. This was the highest award that can be given to an army unit.

At last the 332nd came back to the United States. The War Department recognized its bravery and accomplishments. And indeed the record was a proud one — 111 enemy planes destroyed in the air, 150 more on the ground. The group also destroyed 45 enemy trains and damaged 69 others.

Their skill and daring made all the Red Tails outstanding as pilots and as Americans. They cut a path of honor for those who would follow in America's fighting forces. Never again would an American army have its soldiers live and work separately because of their color . The country had learned an important lesson from these brave airmen.